2-06

DATE DUE

MAY 1 0 2007	MAY 0 4 2017	
SEP 2 9 2007	MAY 1 9 2017	
JUL 0 2 2008	JUN 2 9 2017	
JUL 0 7 2010	OCT 2 1 2019	
MAY 1 0 2011	NOV 2 9 2019	
DEC 1 2 2011	DEC 1 7 2019	
NOV 0 1 2011	FEB 0 3 2020	
FEB 2 8 2013		
JUN 2 9 2016		

DEMCO 128-5046

A
Rookie
reader®

Written by Cari Meister
Illustrated by Terry Sirrell

Children's Press®
A Division of Scholastic Inc.
New York • Toronto • London • Auckland • Sydney
Mexico City • New Delhi • Hong Kong
Danbury, Connecticut

For Peter and Anika
—C.M.

For my seven-year-old daughter Flynn, who thinks
chocolate grows on trees and that they're fun to climb on.
—T.S.

Reading Consultants
Linda Cornwell
Literacy Specialist

Katharine A. Kane
Education Consultant
(Retired, San Diego County Office of Education
and San Diego State University)

Library of Congress Cataloging-in-Publication Data

Meister, Cari.
 I love trees / written by Cari Meister ; illustrated by
Terry Sirrell.
     p. cm. — (A Rookie reader)
Summary: A child lists some of the many things he loves
about trees.
  ISBN 0-516-25900-8 (lib. bdg.)   0-516-26827-9 (pbk.)
 [1. Trees—Fiction. 2. Stories in rhyme.] I. Sirrell,
Terry, ill. II.
Title. III. Series.
PZ8.3.M5514 Im 2004
[E]—dc22
                                2003018656

CHILDREN'S PRESS, and A ROOKIE READER®, and associated logos are trademarks
and or registered trademarks of Scholastic Library Publishing. SCHOLASTIC and
associated logos are trademarks and or registered trademarks of Scholastic Inc.
1 2 3 4 5 6 7 8 9 10 R 13 12 11 10 09 08 07 06 05 04

Trees, trees, trees!

I love trees!

4

Some are big.

Some are tiny.

Some are smooth.

Some are spiny.

9

Some have needles.

10

Some have leaves.

11

Some have birds.

Some have bees!

Some have apples.

Some have pears.

14

Some have owls.

Some have bears!

15

Trees, trees, trees!
I love trees!

They make boats.

They make stables.

They make paper.

They make tables.

They make toys.
They make beds.

They make chairs.

They make sleds.

They make tools.

They make swings.

They make drums.

They make lots of things!

Trees, trees, trees!
I love trees.

WORD LIST (34 WORDS)

apples	drums	owls	tables
are	have	paper	they
bears	I	pears	things
beds	leaves	sleds	tiny
bees	lots	smooth	tools
big	love	some	toys
birds	make	spiny	trees
boats	needles	stables	
chairs	of	swings	

ABOUT THE AUTHOR

Cari Meister lives on a small farm in Minnesota with her husband John, her sons Edwin, Benjamin, and Aaron, their dog Samson, two horses, three cats, two pigs, and two goats. She is the author of more than twenty books for children, including *What Can I Be?*, *I Love Rocks*, *Game Day*, and *A New Roof* in the A Rookie Reader® series.

ABOUT THE ILLUSTRATOR

Cartoonist and illustrator Terry Sirrell has been drawing since 1983. You might have seen his work on the back of Cap'n Crunch and Kellogg's Corn Flakes cereal boxes. His cartoons and characters have also appeared in dozens of publications including *Reader's Digest*, *Newsweek*, *Field and Stream*, *Woman's Day*, *The New York Daily News*, and *The Chicago Tribune*. Terry also illustrates children's books, such as *I Love Rocks* for Children's Press.